Insight from travelers

"Sometimes a book comes along that just knocks it out of the park—and this is one of those reads! I love how Christi weaves in the lives of every-day people of the Bible, to put flesh and skin on the principles of truth. I hope a group study guide will be coming along soon to partner with it!!"

"Don't let this short book fool you. You will embark on a serious study of the scriptures of the lives of many prayerful individuals. I was challenged to dig deeper and truly look at forgiveness and complacency in my own prayer life and refocus on the hope found in Christ. I was encouraged too as I reflected on my own trials how hope was an anchor and praise was the sail that the Lord used to keep me afloat when the storm pressed in."

"Everything I have read from (Christi) has made me thirst more for Jesus and pointed me right where to find Him, in his Word. I was so excited to hear about this book. After reading it, I am overwhelmed! Such real and practical steps to find your way into or back into our heavenly Father's arms."

"This small book is PACKED with fresh insights into old stories from scripture plus quotes and phraseology that will make you stop and think! You may find yourself wanting to share aloud to anyone nearby."

"On the surface, it looks simple and straightforward, but there is a lot of depth if you dare to delve in. Some sentences offer a lifetime of insight and experience just tucked away in a little sub-clause, you don't want to gloss over such pearls of wisdom too fast."

"I can say that this is going to be a book that I place on my purchase list and study at least once a year (much like I do Karen Ehman: Keep It Shut). It instantly caught my attention ... I wanted to take notes, as I usually do when I am truly growing from Christian personal growth books. This book is inspirational and encourages you to renew your relationship with the Lord, it's practical and biblical."

"When I came across a sentence or phrase that I wanted to remember or felt particularly relevant to me, I highlighted it – soon, however, there was so much highlighting that I stopped and just counted everything as relevant."

Revival

6 STEPS TO REVIVING YOUR HEART AND REBUILDING YOUR PRAYER LIFE

CHRISTI GEE

FOR ADDITIONAL RESOURCES &
FREE DOWNLOADS:
REVIVALPRAY.COM/FREE

REVIVAL: 6 STEPS TO REVIVING YOUR HEART AND REBUILDING YOUR PRAYER LIFE

Published by Christi Gee (Make It Count Ink)
Printed in the United States of America

ISBN: 978-1547109494

Discounted Print Copies
Christi Gee is also available to speak to groups on this topic. Special discounts on this book and other related materials for attendees can be considered as part of the speaking package.
To order print copies, start the conversation about a speaking engagement, or inquire about discounted pricing for churches, associations, and other groups, visit RevivalPray.com.

Just for you! Find additional resources that complement this book at RevivalPray.com/free.

To my husband and man of few words.
In you I see the truth of James chapter one
reflected every day.

CONTENTS

Foreword ix

Share the Journey xiii

Preface xv

INTRODUCTION

6 Steps 3

Rebuilding & Revival 7

STEP 1: CLEARING THE RUBBLE

Repent & Forgive 17

Four Things to Pray 27

STEP 2: STABILIZING THE SITE

Recalibrate Your Perspective 39

Lord, Open My Eyes 51

STEP 3: SECURING THE FOUNDATION

Recall God's Sovereignty 57

Three Scriptures to Reflect on in Prayer 67

STEP 4: BUILDING THE WALLS

Recenter Your Hope 77

Three Hope-filled Prayer Prompts 89

STEP 5: SHORING UP THE STRUCTURE

Reinforce with Praise 97

Finding Your Voice Before God 105

STEP 6: STANDING ON THE WALL

Resolve to Shine 115

Three Prayers to Shine and Stand 127

Final Thoughts 133
About the Author 137
How you can help 139
RevivalPray.com 141

FOREWORD

Decades ago one of my favorite groups, Phillips Craig and Dean, released a song titled, *"Will You Love Jesus More?"*

The song begins by listing many ways the writer could have focused your eyes on him, but in the end declares that if all he did was point to himself, he failed.

That song never topped the charts nor made a big splash. But it lived on in my head.

Here, almost 25 years later, it is the best reflection of where my thoughts are as I release this book.

Anyone who knows me can attest that words are my thing. I love turning phrases and pushing alliteration to its limits. The cutting floor for this book is as large as what's here that made the cut. (See what I did there?)

But I intentionally kept *Revival* short for two reasons.

1- I know how stretched your time is.

I know you think you can't add "one more thing."

So I want it to look short.

I want it to look doable.

I want you to think, "Oh, that's not going to overwhelm me at all."

Because I know what's in here and I believe it could usher you before the throne and into God's presence.

And that's the second thing.

2- It's not about me.

Oh, I strung some sentences together, harmonized Scripture for you, and organized it all around a catchy framework. But only to point you to the only One worthy of your attention.

I love talking about the Bible and would have loved to write more. But that would have kept you reading my words instead of getting on with the business of praying.

So instead, I got in, made a point, and got out. And now — tag, you are it.

Dear friend, reader, and fellow journeyer, I am praying for you as I release this book, even though we've never met.

I am praying that when all is said and done, it is not my name you remember. I want you to see Jesus and I want you to love him more.

Making Life & Words Count,

Christi

P.S. If you get a chance, find that song on YouTube. I think you'll love it like I do!

SHARE THE JOURNEY

In today's social age, many love to connect with others while they read.

The following will make it easier for you to find fellow travelers who are sharing this journey, as well as allow me to "hear" you along the way.

Twitter & Instagram:
Use #RevivalPrayBook
Mention/Tag @ChristiLGee

Facebook:
Tag @ChristiGeeDotCom

There's also a special page with easily tweetable quotes and images you're free to download and post:

RevivalPray.com/Quotes

Let's do this together!

PREFACE

This is your warning. You signed up for a fight.

Prayer is powerful. And praying with purpose — grounded in truth from God's Word — will result in renewal, revival, and regaining ground the enemy has stolen.

So do you think his forces are going to allow that to happen without a battle? Not on your life.

When I think of the word **Revival** landing in the enemy's camp, I imagine a nuclear meltdown siren going off, as Satan's demons martial everything they have to come against anyone who dares to think they could experience the "R" word.

If you're intent on rebuilding your prayer life, you must know something: Don't be surprised if it is hard or gets harder.

But remember this: you're not alone. The Lord of Hosts who drew you here will stand guard over your heart. Entreat him now to guide you on this journey of rebuilding and revival.

My verse for the last seven years has been Micah 7:7:

> *"But as for me, I will watch expectantly for the Lord;*
> *I will wait for the God of my salvation.*
> *My God will hear me."*
> (NASB)

Friend, our God WILL hear us. We must watch expectantly for him to answer and act.

Are you ready?

Let's get started!

INTRODUCTION

...

"Christians in revival are accordingly
found living in God's presence,
attending to His Word,
feeling acute concern about sin and righteousness,
rejoicing in the assurance of Christ's love
and their own salvation,
spontaneously constant in worship,
and tirelessly active in witness and service,
fueling these activities by praise and prayer."
—J.I. Packer

6 STEPS

The inspiration for this prayer process is rooted in Nehemiah's rebuilding project that led to the people's revival.

Thus, each prayer step has a related building project theme. Here's the blueprint for our construction plan.

STEP 1

CLEARING THE RUBBLE from the building site is a crucial first step. You must remove trash, dead trees, rocks, and stones that will hinder you from moving forward to level the land and create a foundation worth building upon.

No one applauds the work done at this stage, but it is necessary if you want to prep the site. So it is with this first prayer step of repenting and forgiving. It's not easy. It's not glamorous. But everything else hinges on doing this dirty work.

...

STEP 2

Once the rubble has been cleared the work centers on **STABILIZING THE SITE.** The ground is leveled and graded to ensure the foundation rests on a stable base.

This is also true when you are trying to recover from a trial, endure hardship, or make sense of the non-sensible. You need stabilizing so you can view everything else correctly. This step will help you *recalibrate your perspective.*

...

STEP 3

SECURING THE FOUNDATION comes next. As a prayer warrior, you will lay your cornerstone as you *recall God's sovereignty.*

A right view of God's place in this world and in your life will guard against cracks in your walls and chinks in your armor.

...

STEP 4

Once the foundation is secure, the construction shifts to **BUILDING THE WALLS.** The framework holds up the structure in the middle of a storm.

The framework for this rebuilding and revival project is the hope available through Jesus. This is not just theology; this is lifeology. Without hope, you won't move forward, stand, or even withstand.

So in this step, you will *recenter your hope.*

...

STEP 5

SHORING UP THE STRUCTURE comes next. One of the most powerful strengthening agents for the Christian is praise. It strengthens your ability to endure and calls upon the God who is worthy of your trust.

This step will lead you to *reinforce with praise.*

...

Step 6

You don't experience revival just for yourself. You're called to inspire and prompt others. That's why this last step is called: *resolve to shine.*

There's a dark world out there, and you need to "Let your little light shine." You'll be prepared to spread light and hope as you **STAND ON THE WALL** you have built in the other steps.

DON'T MISS THE BONUS DOWNLOADS AND ADDITIONAL RESOURCES FREE TO YOU WITH THE PURCHASE OF THIS BOOK!

Get your companion Workbook & Prayer Journal at RevivalPray.com/free

REBUILDING & REVIVAL

The stone wall lay in ruins. The people were in *great trouble and shame*. (Neh. 1:3)

When the news reached Nehemiah, Scripture records:

> " *As soon as I heard these words I sat down and wept and mourned for days, and I continued fasting and praying before the God of heaven.*"
> (Neh. 1:4)

The book of Nehemiah is named after the leader who inspired God's people to rebuild their broken wall and convicted them to restore their broken worship.

A century before Nehemiah's time, God allowed the Babylonians to conquer his people (the Israelites — later called Jews) and carry the survivors into captivity. When the Persians overthrew the Babylonians, God used King Cyrus to release the Jews who desired to return to their homeland.

They returned to rebuild their capital city, Jerusalem. In their absence, however, their land had been populated with a myriad of competing cultures and groups who did not want them to succeed.

So there they were. In the middle of a land that used to be theirs. They were a remnant, living amidst pagans who would have loved to see them disappear.

Every day, from every direction, they faced moral and religious challenges that threatened to dilute their distinctive beliefs.

Their leaders took advantage of them, exploiting their brothers and sisters for their own gain. This extortion wounded their morale even worse than the enemy's opposition.

Furthermore, they were trying to reestablish their worship and way of life in the middle of ruins. Without a stone wall around their homes and families, they were vulnerable to attacks from their enemies. **They needed the fortification but felt powerless to make it happen.**

When news of their broken state reached Nehemiah, he was moved with empathy and compassion. He had stayed in Babylon as cupbearer to the king, but his heart was in Jerusalem with his people.

So he fasted and prayed and asked God for permission to be part of the solution. God said "yes" and moved the king to answer likewise.

Nehemiah returned to Jerusalem to fortify the city. When the enemies heard of the rebuilding effort, they were furious. They attacked Nehemiah's character, challenged his patriotism, and openly insinuated that he was a threat to the governing nation. They mocked the progress, demoralized the people, and threatened the workers.

Nehemiah was unmoved. He withstood attacks from the enemies and stood up to the corrupt Jewish elite. He called out sin for what it was. He led the people to both pray and work. He admonished them to defend each other and eased their fears by pointing them back to God.

"Do not be afraid of them.
Remember the Lord,
who is great and awesome,
and fight for your brothers, your sons, your daughters, your
wives, and your homes."
(Neh. 4:14)

Prayer was always Nehemiah's first strategy, but it rarely stood alone. Here, his prayer was paired with setting a guard. He trusted God to protect but knew he was also called to prepare for an enemy attack.

So the people continued to work.

This resulted in a record-breaking building campaign. The stone wall that had laid in ruins for 120 years was rebuilt in 52 days. What came next is perhaps even more notable:

1-The enemies of God's people lost their confidence:

"... for they recognized that this work had been accomplished
with the help of our God."
(Neh. 6:16, NASB)

2-God's people experienced revival.

Revival is always marked with an awareness of sin and a recommitment to God's ways. They actually ASKED the scribe, Ezra, to read from the book of law. They stood and listened for hours. Their listening turned into weeping of repentance when they came face to face with their sins. (Neh. 8)

Their rebuilding led to their revival.

If you need revival in your life, your home, your community, and yes — your nation, this prayer journey is for you.

We are reminded by this story of the difference one person can make.

- One person filled with a holy discontent for the disintegrating status quo.
- One concerned citizen declaring #NotOnMyWatch.
- One prayer warrior confessing sin and requesting a commission.
- One person receiving a God-ordained assignment.

ONE LAST THING:
PRAY IT FORWARD

———————

Let's travel back to Nehemiah's commission. When he initially heard, wept, and prayed over the state of Jerusalem, that was in the fall of one year.

His prayer ended like this:

> *"O Lord, please hear my prayer! ...*
> *grant me success today*
> *by making the king favorable to me..."*
> (Neh. 1:11, NLT)

God began answering, but Nehemiah didn't see the evidence until the following Spring. That Spring he was serving King Artaxerxes and Nehemiah's face reflected his pain over the state of his people. Scripture records the king opened the conversation, asking Nehemiah how he could help.

Look at what Nehemiah said about his answer:

> *"With a prayer to the God of heaven, I replied,*
> *'If it please the king ...*

send me to Judah to rebuild the city
where my ancestors are buried.'"
(Neh. 2:4-5, NLT)

Think about that opening statement: **"With a prayer to the God of heaven, I replied."**

When the king asked, "How can I help you?" Nehemiah saw it as his prayer answer and responded in faith as he continued to pray. In Nehemiah, we see this truth:

Ceaseless prayer creates operational courage.

Nehemiah didn't stop to pray. Nor did he move forward on his own.

He "prayed it forward" as he *acted* on what had already been *percolating* in his prayers.

If you enter seriously into focused prayer before God, based on his Word, you can expect him to work.

So I challenge you right here and now to commit to each step of this journey. And then be ready to *Pray it Forward* when God answers your earnest pleas.

Revival

NOTES

THOUGHTS

prayers

STEP 1: CLEARING THE RUBBLE

...

"If you are renewed by grace, and were to meet your old self, I am sure you would be very anxious to get out of his company."
— Charles H. Spurgeon

REPENT &
FORGIVE

Two Pillar Concepts

Clearing the land is an important part of getting ready to build. You must remove trash, dead trees, and rocks that will hinder your progress in leveling the ground.

So it is with confession and repentance. No one applauds the work done at this stage, but it is vital if we want to experience spiritual awakening.

Repentance MOVES our God
and it launches Revivals.

Everything else crumbles if we don't first clear the rubble from our hearts. We do this by pausing to consider, confess, repent, and reset.

Before we dive into how this step applies to us, let's look at what God chose to have recorded in Scripture that reflects the importance he places on this act of obedience. Here are two pillar thoughts about repentance:

> ## 1. REPENTANCE IS ASSOCIATED WITH ENTERING GOD'S PRESENCE.

For this first concept, let's consider three examples from Scripture displayed in the prayers of Jesus, Nehemiah, and David.

♦ JESUS ♦

When Jesus was teaching his disciples how to pray, he modeled some basic tenets (Matt. 6:9-13).

1. Glory to God's name (v 9)
2. Submission to his kingdom (v 10)
3. Submission to his will (v 10)
4. Request provision (v 11)
5. Request forgiveness (v 12)
6. Give forgiveness (v 12)
7. Request strength from temptation (v 13)
8. Request deliverance from evil (v 13)

Some commentators divide this list into only six sections. However you slice and dice it, repentance and forgiveness make up a hefty component of this model. The importance of forgiveness and being forgiven is the one concept that is reiterated by Jesus in this same teaching. [1] More on that later.

♦ Nehemiah ♦

When Nehemiah asked God to hear his pleas, his prayer included confession. In a sandwich-type form, he prayed:

1. Hear my prayer
"let your ear be attentive and your eyes open, to hear the prayer of your servant ..."
(Neh. 1:6a)

2. We have sinned

"... confessing the sins of the people of Israel, which we have sinned against you. Even I and my father's house have sinned. We have acted very corruptly against you..."

(Neh. 1:6b-7)

3. Hear my prayer

"O Lord, let your ear be attentive to the prayer of your servant..."

(Neh. 1:11a)

God used this prayer to launch a movement and restore his people. It's not a coincidence that Nehemiah was moved to admit his sin and that of his people before God used him to lead others to revival.

♦ DAVID ♦

Another example is found in King David's confession following his adultery with Bathsheba. He wrote Psalm 51 after the prophet Nathan confronted his sin. One of the hallmarks of Psalm 51 is verse 10:

> *"Create in me a clean heart, O God,*
> *and renew a right spirit within me."*

The next verse goes on to plead:

> *"Cast me not away from your presence,*
> *and take not your Holy Spirit from me."*

There's something there that teaches us David recognized that his sin — prior to his repentance — had created distance between God and him.

John MacArthur summarizes Psalm 51 this way:
"Sin had made him dirty and he wanted to be clean. Guilt had made him sick and he wanted to be well. Disobedience had made him lonely and he wanted to be reconciled. Rebellion had made him fearful and he wanted to be pardoned." [2]

Gills Exposition Commentary notes:
"The people of God are never cast away from his favour, or out of his heart's love; but they may for a while be without his gracious presence, or not see his face, nor have the light of his countenance, nor sensible communion with him ... By sin, the Spirit of God may be grieved, so as to withdraw his gracious influences, and his powerful operations may not be felt ..." [3]

2. REVIVAL IS MARKED BY REPENTANCE

Scripture also shows us how repentance both lays the foundation for and marks the occasion of revival. Consider two more examples from Scripture:

♦ NEHEMIAH ♦

In the story of Nehemiah's rebuilding effort, we read that after the wall was finished, revival broke out (Neh. 8). It began with weeping and repentance in response to the Word being read and understood.

The people asked Ezra to read God's Word and they stood listening from early morning until midday. Scripture records that the ears of all the people were attentive. They bowed their heads and worshiped the Lord with their faces to the ground, and they wept as they listened.

From there, they continued to read the Law and reinstated the feasts and rituals commanded by God.

This culminated in another session of corporate listening and confession. Nehemiah 9 records they spent three hours reading the law and being reminded from the chronicles of history of the sins of their forefathers. They then spent another three hours confessing their part in the sin of their nation.

Revival followed their rebuilding and it began with — and was advanced by — repentance.

♦ DANIEL ♦

Before Nehemiah's time, Daniel held influence in the Persian government. After reading the prophecies, he realized the time was drawing near for God to act and release his people from captivity. He was compelled to intercede and his prayer is recorded in Daniel 9.

Before he asked God to move on behalf of Israel, he first confessed his sin and the sin of the people.

God did move. The people were set free from captivity and went on to experience revival in their homeland.

Revival is marked by a profound consciousness of sin. When the Holy God of all creation draws near, we become even more aware of how unworthy we are of his presence.

Few things bring you closer to the heart of God than an earnest plea that He would prick your heart, call you to repentance, and wash you whiter than snow. And when you are through the hard work of confession and repentance, there is joy and favor to be enjoyed.

———

...

"Repentance, not proper behaviour or even holiness, is the doorway to grace. And the opposite of sin is grace, not virtue."
— Phillip Yancey [4]

...

"When may a revival be expected? When the wickedness of the wicked grieves and distresses the Christian."
— Billy Sunday [5]

...

———

NOTES

1. *"For if you forgive others their trespasses, your heavenly Father will also forgive you, but if you do not forgive others their trespasses, neither will your Father forgive your trespasses."* (Matt. 6:14-15)

2. http://www.gty.org/resources/sermons/80-353/the-believers-confession-of-sin

3. http://biblehub.com/commentaries/gill/psalms/51.htm

4. Philip Yancey, *What's So Amazing About Grace?* (Grand Rapids, Michigan: Zondervan, 1997).

5. William T. Ellis, *Billy Sunday, the Man and His Message* (Philadelphia, Pennsylvania: The John C. Winston Company, 1917), 293.

FOUR THINGS TO PRAY

———~~~———

A Rubble-Clearing, Revival-Starting,
Repentance-Marking Prayer

When we combine the examples of Jesus, Nehemiah, Daniel, and David, a four-prong prayer bubbles to the surface. Here's a suggestion for what to pray on this rubble-clearing day.

1-ASK GOD FOR A HOLY DISCONTENT.

Ask him to remove any complacency about the status quo in your life, your home, and your community. Ask

27

him to substitute in compassion and empathy for others held captive to sin.

Think about Nehemiah's immediate response to the news about his people:

> *"As soon as I heard these words*
> *I sat down and wept and mourned for days,*
> *and I continued fasting and praying*
> *before the God of heaven."*
> (Neh. 1:4)

Daniel's prayer mentioned earlier begins with this description:

> *"Then I turned my face to the Lord God,*
> *seeking him by prayer and pleas for mercy*
> *with fasting and sackcloth and ashes."*
> (Dan. 9:3)

These are examples of holy discontent. Ask God to show you what isn't right and what is worthy of your heart-filled, holy-inspired grief.

When you ask for this, you'll likely become aware of sin in your life that needs to be confessed. So that's the second prong.

2-CONFESS KNOWN SIN AND REPENT.

As a believer, you've embraced the Gospel. The reason the Gospel is such good news is because:

"... all have sinned and fall short of the glory of God."
(Rom. 3:23)

You are redeemed, but not yet perfect. Confession reflects that you know this, which is a mark of a true believer.

"But if we walk in the light,
as he is in the light,
we have fellowship with one another,
and the blood of Jesus his Son cleanses us from all sin.

If we say we have no sin,
we deceive ourselves,
and the truth is not in us.

If we confess our sins,
he is faithful and just to forgive us our sins
and to cleanse us from all unrighteousness.

If we say we have not sinned,
we make him a liar,

and his word is not in us."
(1 John 1:8-10)

A genuine Christian walks habitually in the light, not in darkness. This walk results in cleansing from sin as the Lord continually forgives his own.

> Confession of sin
> characterizes genuine Christians,
> and God continually cleanses
> those who are confessing.
> Those who are confessing
> are always walking in the light
> and continually being cleansed.
> The two are inter-related. [1]

Confession is saying the same thing about sin as God does and acknowledging his perspective about sin. Repentance is turning from that sin — forsaking it and leaving it behind.

Confess, repent, and ask God to show you what you're overlooking. And trust that as you continue to walk in the light, he will continue to cleanse you.

Amen! Isn't that a sweet promise? But wait, there's more.

Nehemiah and Daniel gave examples of confession that wasn't just for their own personal sins. They both fell to their knees weeping over sin they didn't directly commit.

Although you cannot receive forgiveness for others or take the place of their responsibility to repent, you can intercede on their behalf. God calls believers to enter into each other's trials and troubles.

So as you pray for your own sins and shortcomings, ask God for a heart full of empathy and discernment to pray for others trapped by the enemy and their own flesh. The weight of sin that entangles is often too hard to throw off alone.

3- FORGIVE OTHERS.

The same Gospel lens you apply to your own sin is the lens you have to use as you look at friends and family. "For all fall short of the glory of God" applies to us all.

God has already warned you about them and he's warned them about you. When you remember that truth, you will be more prepared to forgive.

We looked at the *Lord's Prayer* earlier. Jesus closed that session by emphasizing one aspect he had modeled. He didn't add commentary to bringing glory to God or asking for his will. The one thing he chose to elaborate on was forgiveness:

"For if you forgive others their trespasses, your heavenly Father will also forgive you,

but if you do not forgive others their trespasses, neither will your Father forgive your trespasses."
(Matt. 6:14-15)

C.S. Lewis said, "To be a Christian means to forgive the inexcusable because God has forgiven the inexcusable in you." [2]

Corrie ten Boom said, "Forgiveness is an act of the will, and the will can function regardless of the temperature of the heart." [3]

It's worth noting that the act of forgiving someone who has not asked for your forgiveness is — well, to put it plainly — hard. Furthermore, if the transgression against you cut deeply or the hurt is still fresh, you'll need an extra measure of strength to follow through on forgiving. This will only be accomplished through the power of prayer and the intercession of the Holy Spirit. If this is something you are struggling with, remember you need to ask God for his power to enable and sustain your forgiveness. You may even have to start with this plea, "Lord, help me WANT to want to forgive."

When my friend edited this book for me, she sent back this insight. I know she didn't intend for me to add it, but I just have to share her wisdom:

"When I can't pray for someone who has hurt me, I do what my mother told me:
'Pray for their mother." It works. I eventually end up praying for the person."

4- ASK GOD TO RESTORE THE JOY OF YOUR SALVATION.

In the story of revival recorded in Nehemiah 8, we saw how the people wept over their sin initially. It is in the middle of this weeping over sin that an often-quoted verse finds its context:

33

"This day is holy to the Lord your God;
do not mourn or weep.
And do not be grieved,
for the joy of the Lord is your strength."
(Neh. 8:10)

The words the people heard reminded them God punishes sin, but Nehemiah reminded them that God also blesses obedience. That was a reason to celebrate. They had not been utterly destroyed as a nation, in spite of their sin. God still had a plan for them.

David's confession and repentance in Psalm 51 ended with this plea:

"Restore to me the joy of your salvation,
and uphold me with a willing spirit."
(Ps. 51:12)

So ask God to restore the joy of your salvation. It is good news that you can repent and be cleansed and rely on the Lord for your strength and your joy.

"For his anger is but for a moment,
and his favor is for a lifetime.
Weeping may tarry for the night,
but joy comes with the morning."
(Ps. 30:5)

34

Revival

NOTES

THOUGHTS

prayers

NOTES

1. *The MacArthur Study Bible*, New American Standard (Nashville, Tennessee: Thomas Nelson, Inc., 2006), 1934.

2. C.S. Lewis, *The Weight of Glory* (New York: Harper Collins, 2001: Originally published 1949), 181-183.

3. *Guideposts* (Carmel, New York, 1972).

STEP 2:
STABILIZING
THE SITE

...

"When matters are taken out of your hands, never conclude
they've been taken out of God's hands."
— Carey Nieuwhof

RECALIBRATE YOUR PERSPECTIVE

Two Stories | Two Takeaways

Once the rubble has been cleared for a building project the ground must be graded. The level ground will ensure the foundation rests on a stable base.

So it is with us when we are trying to recover from a trial, endure hardship, or make sense of the non-sensible. We need to be stabilized so we view everything else correctly.

I learned this first hand. Through my own trial, my head kept reciting truth from God's Word about his sovereignty and perfect plan. But the veins that carried that truth to my heart were clogged. I wanted to believe the truth about his power, but I first needed the reassurance of his presence.

God never left my side; he was always near. The same is true for you. However, if our eyes have been focused on the wrong things — like the mounting problem, declining culture, or deteriorating condition, then we may have a cloudy view.

That's why this second step involves recalibrating your perspective. To prepare your mind for prayer, we'll look at two stories of God's presence and two takeaways about perspective.

TWO STORIES OF GOD'S PRESENCE

◆ ELIJAH ◆

1 Kings 19 records the prophet Elijah's meltdown. After his victory on Mount Carmel (ch. 18), Queen Jezebel declared Elijah to be a *dead man walking*.

Elijah ran for his life. He went into the wilderness and asked God to let him die. God appeared and asked, "What are you doing here, Elijah?"

Elijah replied:

> *"I have been very jealous for the Lord, the God of hosts.*
> *For the people of Israel have forsaken your covenant,*
> *thrown down your altars,*
> *and killed your prophets with the sword,*
> *and I, even I only, am left,*
> *and they seek my life, to take it away."*
> (1 Kings 19:10)

Elijah told God he was the only one left and indicated he failed to see that anything good had come in Israel from his zealous efforts for the Lord.

After God took care of Elijah's physical needs, he gave him the gift of himself: both his presence and his perspective.

God told Elijah to go stand on the mountain. Three times a great phenomenon occurred. First came a wind so strong it broke pieces of the mountain off. An earthquake and then a fire followed. Each time, the Bible records God was not in those.

Then came the sound of a gentle blowing, and God's voice was in the faint whisper. Elijah was shown that the Almighty God is always at work, even if it is imperceptible to human eyes.

After giving Elijah his presence, God gave him a perspective shift. He told Elijah he had reserved 7,000 in Israel for himself. Elijah wasn't the only one left and God still had a job for Elijah in his plan.

Furthermore, God told Elijah he wasn't going solo ever again. He told him to find Elisha and anoint him as a fellow prophet. And from then on —until Elijah was taken up in a whirlwind into heaven— he was never alone doing God's work again.

Part of Elijah's problem could be summed up in his loss of perspective. **He lost sight of God's bigger picture when he started listening to the smaller ruler Jezebel.**

His perspective was recalibrated when he was assured of God's presence. That's what you're doing with this day of prayer: opening your eyes to the reality of God's presence in your life and his promises of being near.

The second story revolves around opened eyes.

♦ ELISHA ♦

Elijah's companion, Elisha, has his own story to contribute to our study (2 Kings 6).

Elisha supplied the king of Israel inside-intel on his enemy, the king of Syria. As you might expect, this marked Elisha as "most wanted" by the Syrian king. One night Syrian horses and chariots surrounded the city where Elisha and his servant were stationed. When the servant rose early the next morning, he could see the enemy in full force encircled around the city. Distraught, he asked Elisha what they should do.

Elisha responded to his servant:

> *"Do not fear, for those who are with us are more than those who are with them."*

Then Elisha prayed and asked God:

> *"O LORD, I pray, open his eyes that he may see."*

43

Scripture records God's answer:

> *"And the LORD opened the servant's eyes*
> *and he saw;*
> *and behold, the mountain was full*
> *of horses and chariots of fire all around Elisha."*
> (2 Kings 6:16-17)

Enlightened, the servant observed the unseen world of God's heavenly armies, waiting to do battle with the enemy. The Syrians had stationed horses and chariots around the city, but the Lord had FILLED the mountains behind them with horses and chariots of FIRE.

Did you notice that Elisha didn't ask God to rescue them? He asked for his servant to understand the reality of the deliverance already in process. The young man could only see the enemy's activity in front of him. **Although the enemy was real, that was only a partial reality.**

These two stories teach the same message about the relationship between God's presence and our perspective.

- Elijah needed the reminder of God's presence to correct his perspective.

- Elisha's servant needed his eyes opened to see what had been there all along.

Often, if your view is skewed, it is likely due in part to one of the following takeaways about perspective.

TWO TAKEAWAYS ABOUT PERSPECTIVE

---

1. DO NOT MISTAKE GOD'S SILENCE FOR ABSENCE

You may be in a time of trials. It may seem that God is distant. Maybe you are being tested by God or attacked by Satan. You may even be fighting your own flesh. It may feel like God doesn't hear your prayers or care about your pain. All around you see evidence of others' answered prayers and wonder if you've been left out.

I don't know why God is silent at times. Yes, it could be unconfessed sin; that's why we started with that in step one. But his ways are not our ways and sometimes he chooses to grow our faith, which by very definition is:

"... the assurance of things hoped for,
the conviction of things not seen."
(Heb. 11:1)

In the movie, <u>God's Not Dead 2</u>, a wise grandfather counsels his teacher-granddaughter who is on trial for her faith and has become weary and discouraged. He reminds her, "Honey, you know as well as anyone, during the test, the teacher is always silent." [1]

Paul knew there would be times when we needed our perspective recalibrated. This is what he prayed for the Ephesians.

"I pray that the eyes of your heart may be enlightened,
so that you will know what is the hope of His calling,
what are the riches of the glory of His inheritance
in the saints,
and what is the surpassing greatness
of His power toward us who believe."
(Eph. 1:18-19)

You too are called to pray that God would open your eyes and enlighten your view of both his presence and his power. He will answer that prayer, but not always on your timeline. So remember this:

**When it comes to faith,
what is seen (or not seen)
cannot trump what is known.**

And that's the second takeaway.

---

2. DON'T LET THE CIRCUMSTANCES SURROUNDING YOU CIRCUMVENT THE TRUTH SUSTAINING YOU.

Whatever is going on in your life is real, but it's not the full reality. Regardless of how big the problem is, your God is always bigger.

And what's more: his omnipotence is matched by his omnipresence. Consider the following verses that remind you of this truth.

As Jesus was about to ascend to heaven, he gave his disciples some final encouragement regarding the work they would complete on his behalf:

"Behold, I am with you always,
to the end of the age."
(Matt. 28:20)

This well-known verse from Philippians 4:6-7 is recited by many:

"Be anxious for nothing, but in everything by prayer and
supplication with thanksgiving let your requests be made
known to God.

And the peace of God, which passes all understanding,
will guard your hearts and your minds in Christ Jesus."

However, the ability to follow the instruction in verse six and rest on the promise in verse seven hinges on the four words at the end of verse five: **The Lord is near.**

The Lord is near. That changes everything.

Faith isn't based on the evidence of answered prayers
but on the promise of a God who hears and is near.

Because the Lord is near, we can have a peace that passes all understanding, even when we can't see the Lord of Hosts' army surrounding us.

...

"The only way you will be able to see life with 20/20 vision is when you look at life from a kingdom perspective."
— Tony Evans [2]

...

"Our awareness of his presence may falter, but the reality of his presence never changes."
— Max Lucado [3]

NOTES

1. Pat Boone as the grandfather, *God's Not Dead 2* (United States, Pure Flix Entertainment, 2016), directed by Harold Cronk.

2. Tony Evans, *The Kingdom Agenda* (Chicago, Illinois: Moody Publishers, 2006), 32.

3. Max Lucado, *Just Like Jesus* (Nashville, Tennessee: Thomas Nelson, 2003), 53.

LORD, OPEN MY EYES

—⁓⁓—

As we end this section with prayer, consider this before the Lord:

How level is your ground?

If your perspective is holding steady and you are walking in peace, thank God for this season of hope and ask him to show you how to trust deeper.

If you are NOT holding steady, consider these questions:

- Are you focusing on the wrong things, thus clouding your view?

- Are you in a spiritual dry season and doubting His nearness?
- Are you in a trial or a storm, and the winds and the waves are drowning your eyes?
- Do you feel like Elijah ("I'm the only one left") or Elisha's servant (all you can see is the enemy)?

Regardless of the reason, the answer is the same: Draw near to God in prayer.

Pray the Scriptures in the previous chapter back to him. Ask him to show you how to draw nearer to him and hold him to his promise to draw near to you. (James 4:8)

♦ A PRAYER TO OPEN YOUR EYES ♦

Oh, Lord of Hosts ~

OPEN MY EYES.

Open my eyes to the reality of your presence.
You are near and you have promised to be with me.

Dispatch that truth to calm my anxious heart.
Send the peace that passes all understanding echoing through my mind.

Show me how to give more of myself over to your Spirit to take hold and transplant hope.

When I feel like I can't go on,
shelter me under your wing and refuel me to walk in faith.
And when I think I am defeated,
turn my thoughts to the cross where you defeated sin and death.

Train me to see the evidence of your power and your presence.
Guard my eyes from focusing on the smaller rulers all around me.
Teach me to see what cannot be seen.
Enable me to stand against the unseen forces that seek to destroy me.

Open my eyes to look beyond the enemy and see the mountains FULL of your FORCES on FIRE.

OPEN MY EYES.

Revival

NOTES

prayers

STEP 3:
SECURING THE
FOUNDATION

...

"This is God's universe, and God does things his way. You may have a better way, but you don't have a universe."
— Vernon McGee

RECALL GOD'S SOVEREIGNTY

Three Examples of Reliance

In the last two chapters, we first cleared the rubble through repentance, and then we leveled the construction site.

You steadied your mind and stabilized your heart by opening your eyes to the reality of God's very real and near presence in your life.

Now you're ready for the Cornerstone — a solid foundation. An accurate view of God's place in this world and in your life will guard against cracks in your walls.

Before we look at three servants who got this right, let's look at two who initially got it wrong, starting with a hero of the faith.

◆ ◆ ◆

When Moses encountered God's presence at the burning bush, it was because God had a mission for Moses to fulfill — delivering the children of Israel out of Egypt. Moses' initial response was, "*Who am I that I should go ...*" (Ex. 3:11)

I heard Priscilla Shirer summarize God's response to Moses as something like this, "It doesn't matter who **YOU** are, Moses. You go tell them who I **AM**!" [1]

By focusing on his own insecurities, Moses forgot to recall God's secure foundation. This wasn't about Moses, although God was graciously drawing him into the story. This was, always had been, and always would be about God's plan, God's glory, and God's power displayed through his people.

That teaching on Exodus entered my world shortly before my own burning bush moment. Weeks after studying that lesson, I was asked to keynote a women's retreat. Although I had spoken for single sessions, I had never written an entire retreat. Everything in me wanted to scurry for cover.

I kept flipping that insight around in my mind like you do a peppermint —trying to get all the flavor out of it. In the end, I knew that message was for me. It didn't matter who I was. I was being called to lead other women into the presence of God.

The weekend went beautifully, but the aftermath in my life was so painful that I vowed to never do that again. The enemy saved the spiritual attacks for AFTER the retreat. It was almost like he said, "Humph, I'll teach you to do THAT again."

Fast forward a few years. Another group asked me to keynote their retreat. By that time, I had recovered enough to say "Yes" initially. However, during the months of preparation, my old enemy returned. Before long, I was drowning in a sea of questions that sounded like, "Who am I to do this? Why did I ever agree? What was I thinking?" Fear settled in and I froze.

Because I couldn't make progress on writing a Bible study, I distracted myself with reading about it. I picked up Jen Wilkin's *Women of the Word* and before I got out of the first chapter, I knew God had met me in a bush — inside a book — again.

She opens her teaching on how to study the Bible by reminding her readers that most people ask the wrong questions. Guess what story she chose to illustrate her point? Yep, Moses and the burning bush.

She notes that God removed Moses totally from the subject of the discussion and inserted himself. The only answer to "Who am I?" was "I am."

"Our insecurities, fears, and doubts
can never be banished by
the knowledge of who we are.
They can only be banished by the knowledge of 'I AM'."
— Jen Wilkin [2]

So there it was again. The burning bush. The wrong questions. And the faithful Author using his children-authors to remind me of the truth authored in his Word. That's a lot of authoring.

Which brings me to one more admission. In trying to push this book to the finish line, I hit the same wall with the same questions. The same fear enveloped me. And for a third time, I experienced the only answer to that fear: it's not about me.

They say third time's the charm. Here's hoping. But I wouldn't place any bets on this servant. (Who, by the way, is the second one who got it wrong I mentioned earlier.) Seems like I'm in good company with my friend Moses; he and I are going to have coffee in heaven. But seriously, I'm thankful for the honest transparency of Scripture that shows how God responds to faith-failures and that he uses us in spite of ourselves.

I'm equally grateful for all the heroic examples that show us what it looks like when your first response is to look to God.

Now we'll turn our attention to the three Old Testament servants we considered previously: Nehemiah, David, and Daniel. We'll look at their examples of relying on God's sovereignty as a FIRST response and not a last resort.

♦ Nehemiah ♦

In Nehemiah's story of the post-captivity rebuilding campaign, we've seen multiple instances of enemy attacks and taunts. At one point, the opposition mounted so heavily against the Jews as they were working on the wall, they lost their confidence, believing they could not go on:

"The strength of those who bear the burdens is failing ..."
(Neh. 4:10)

Nehemiah's answer to their fear and discouragement was NOT to reaffirm their abilities or gifts and talents or build them up inwardly. Instead, he pointed the people upward and renewed their focus on the only one worthy of their attention:

"Do not be afraid of them.
Remember the Lord,
who is great and awesome ..."
(Neh. 4:14)

After reestablishing their focus on God's power, Nehemiah implemented a plan that organized the people and readied them for both work and war. It's worth noticing that he accompanied prayer with a plan, but he first focused on the POWER that sustained that plan.

♦ **DAVID** ♦

The context for Psalm 11 is a national crisis. Some counselors who were panicked approached David. They essentially asked: "In view of a crumbling society, what can one righteous person, out of a shrinking remnant, do?"

David's inspired response was this:

> *"The LORD is in his holy temple;*
> *the Lord's throne is in heaven."*
>
> (Ps. 11:4a)

David's answer emphasized God's sovereignty and the transcendent throne room he occupies.

- This moved the mood from PANIC to PEACE.
- This took the question from ME to HIM.
- This replaced DO with TRUST.

♦ DANIEL ♦

Daniel's prayer (ch. 9) asking God to move on behalf of Israel centered on God's glory and his sovereignty. Consider how many times the word "your" is used in just these four verses:

> *"O Lord, in accordance with all **Your** righteous acts,*
> *let now **Your** anger and **Your** wrath turn away*
> *from **Your** city Jerusalem, **Your** holy mountain;*

63

for because of our sin and the iniquities of our fathers,
*Jerusalem and **Your** people have become a reproach*
to all those around us.
So now, our God, listen to the prayer
*of **Your** servant and to his supplications,*
*and for **Your** sake, O Lord,*
*let **Your** face shine on **Your** desolate sanctuary.*
*O my God, incline **Your** ear and hear!*
*Open **Your** eyes and see our desolations*
*and the city which is called by **Your** name;*
for we are not presenting our supplications
*before **You** on account of any merits of our own,*
*but on account of **Your** great compassion.*
O Lord, hear! O Lord, forgive!
O Lord, listen and take action!
*For **Your** own sake, O my God, do not delay, because **Your***
*city and **Your** people are called by **Your** name."*
(Dan. 9:16-19, NASB)

These three prayer examples reveal godly men focused on the God of the universe who heard their prayers:

- Nehemiah restored courage by pointing the people toward God.
- David replied to panic with the truth that God is NEVER off his throne.
- Daniel entreated God to move with a prayer

centered solely on God's glory, for his name, and for his sake.

The answer is never to work in our own strength or for our own purposes. It's all about God. It's all accomplished according to his power and his will.

If you and I internalize this one truth, letting it guide our actions and reactions, it could transform our journeys. Here's to better questions and greater answers.

———

...

"Oddly, the most freeing thing we can ever do is to abdicate the throne of our own miniature kingdoms."
—Beth Moore [3]

...

*"As Moses would learn during the Exodus, **who he was** bore no impact on the outcome of his situation. **Who God was** made all the difference."*
— Jen Wilkin [4]

...

———

NOTES

1. Pricilla Shirer, *Anointed, Transformed, Redeemed* (Nashville, Tennessee: LifeWay Press, 2008), video teaching session.

2. Jen Wilkin, *Women of the Word: How to Study the Bible with Both our Hearts and our Minds* (Wheaton, Illinois: Crossway, 2014), 26

3. Beth Moore, *Esther: It's Tough Being a Woman* (Nashville, Tennessee: Lifeway Press, 2008), 18.

4. Wilkin, 27.

THREE
SCRIPTURES TO
REFLECT ON IN
PRAYER

⌁⌁⌁

As you seek to make forward progress in rebuilding your prayer life and reviving your heart, you are certain to encounter opposition. Throughout Scripture (and especially the Psalms), we see how an awareness of God's sovereignty over all creation is the answer for anyone who is struggling with fear, discouragement, worry, etc.

It is the same for you. Recalling and reflecting on God's power and his steadfast love and faithfulness is a powerful defense against the enemy who stalks your peace.

Take these three passages before the Lord in prayer and ask him to exchange your panic for peace, your striving for trusting, and your focus on what you cannot do for an awareness of what he has already done.

1. PSALM 115:1-3

(1) *Not to us, O LORD, not to us, but to your name give glory, for the sake of your steadfast love and your faithfulness!*
(2) *Why should the nations say, "Where is their God?"*
(3) *Our God is in the heavens; he does all that he pleases."*

Consider the following:

Verse 1 repeats "not to us" twice and three times the word "your" is used: your name, your love, your faithfulness.
Verse 2 is a Gentile taunt to the Jewish people regarding their God and their faith in that God.
Verse 3 is the answer to this taunt. Think about what is NOT included in this answer, and how often our

responses to challenges to our faith include a laundry list of replies.

Pray verse 1 and 3 back to God.

---

2. ROMANS 11:33-12:2

(11:33-36)
Oh, the depth of the riches and wisdom and knowledge of God!
How unsearchable are his judgments
and how inscrutable his ways!
"For who has known the mind of the Lord,
or who has been his counselor?"
"Or who has given a gift to him that he might be repaid?"
For from him and through him and to him are all things.
To him be glory forever. Amen.

(12:1-2)
I appeal to you therefore, brothers, by the mercies of God,
to present your bodies as a living sacrifice,
holy and acceptable to God,
which is your spiritual worship.
Do not be conformed to this world,
but be transformed by the renewal of your mind,

that by testing you may discern what is the will of God,
what is good and acceptable and perfect.

You are likely familiar with 12:1 "...present your bodies a living and holy sacrifice ..." and 12:2 "do not be conformed to this world ..." But have you noticed this passage includes a "therefore" in the beginning?

In Scripture, when you see "therefore," you must ask, "What is 'therefore' there for?" The answer lies in the preceding verses (11:33-36).

Contemplate before God how embracing the truth at the end of chapter 11 will enable you to live out the commands in the beginning of chapter 12.

Pray 11:33-36 as a direct prayer, simply changing instances of "him/his" to "you/your."

---

3. PSALM 46

Psalm 46:10 is a favorite verse of many:

"Be still, and know that I am God." (ESV)
"Cease striving and know..." (NASB)

This peaceful instruction in verse 10 is preceded by nine verses that are the foundation for why you can, indeed, cease striving and be still, in full assurance that God is God.

In essence, the message is that regardless of what collapses around you:

- Because God is your STRENGTH, you can be STILL.
- Because God is your REFUGE, you will not be MOVED.
- Because God is your FORTRESS, you can know HE will be EXALTED.

Specifically consider the name of God used in verses 7 and 11: Lord of Hosts. This is Jehovah Sabaoth, also translated "The Lord of Armies," and it is used over 270 times in the Bible, most frequently in Isaiah and Jeremiah. Isaiah and Jeremiah were prophets who warned God's people of the impending destruction if they did not return to God during the pre-captivity time. [1]

This name "Lord of Hosts" denotes God's universal sovereignty over every army — both spiritual and earthly — and reminds us he commands a host of angels "that excel in strength, that do his commandments" (Ps. 103:20).

The Lord of Hosts is sovereign over your nation.
The Lord of Hosts is sovereign over your church.
The Lord of Hosts is sovereign over your family.
The Lord of Hosts is sovereign over your heart.

The Lord of HOSTS is WITH YOU!

Note: The artists Shane & Shane put this Psalm to music. The recording is beautiful and will usher your heart into worship. Find it on YouTube by searching "Shane & Shane Psalm 46".

Revival

NOTES

THOUGHTS

prayers

NOTES

1. Michael Gowens, *A Study of God's Hebrew Names* (Shallotte, North Carolina: Sovereign Grace Publications, 2016), 179.

STEP 4: BUILDING THE WALLS

...

Hope as an anchor to the soul. What an image!
(based on Heb. 6:19)

RECENTER YOUR HOPE

Built on Nothing Less

The framework is essential for any building project. It's what everything attaches to and it's what holds up the structure in the middle of a storm.

The framework for this rebuilding and revival project is Jesus and the hope of your home in heaven. Everything about your place and your part in life builds on this truth:

Jesus died for your sin, rose again,
and is coming back one day to take you home.

The Gospel is not just theology; it is lifeology.

You will work harder, love deeper, and forgive sooner if you keep your eyes fixed on heaven and the one who made heaven possible for you.

Hope fuels life. Without hope, you won't move forward, stand, or even withstand. Thus, sometimes it becomes necessary to RECENTER your HOPE, and that's what we're doing in this step. You're going to see from Scripture how the writers of the New Testament and Jesus himself believed this hope — awareness and anticipation of Jesus' return — was the KEY to walking in faith.

RECENTER YOUR HOPE ON JESUS

Your hope source is directly tied to where your eyes focus. So, recentering your hope could alternately be called "fixing your eyes."

> *"Therefore, since we have so great a*
> *cloud of witnesses surrounding us,*

let us also lay aside every encumbrance
and the sin which so easily entangles us,
and let us run with endurance
the race that is set before us,
fixing our eyes on Jesus,
the author and perfecter of faith,
who for the joy set before Him endured the cross,
despising the shame,
and has sat down at the right hand
of the throne of God."
(Heb. 12:1-2, NASB)

According to the author of Hebrews, where you fix your eyes is the key to moving forward and running your race with endurance.

I've illustrated this with children by having them walk forward while looking behind, down, or to the side. Rarely can they reach the intended target I laid out in front of them.

The same is true with our spiritual journey forward. We need our eyes to move forward safely and to hit our target. But it's not just about having our eyes opened and unblinded; it's about focusing on the right thing.

We know the "what" of the right thing: Jesus. But HOW do we do that? The author of Hebrews seemed to have an idea.

We fix our eyes on Jesus by focusing on how he is both:
... the founder and the finisher
... the starter and the closer
... the author and perfecter
of our faith.

Here's how this plays out practically.

FIX YOUR EYES ON JESUS AS:
AUTHOR OF YOUR FAITH

If you will make it a priority to dwell — and dwell often — on Jesus as the AUTHOR of your faith and on the truth that God saved you, it will transform your daily walk.

The more you call to mind the truth found in Ephesians 1 — that **he chose** you in him before the foundation of the world was laid and predestined you to be like Jesus — the more you realize it is **NOT all up to you,** and it's not all about you. You didn't earn it and you can't burn it.

The outgrowth of this meditation will be an overflowing of grace that floods your soul and fixes your eyes like a laser on your Savior.

Consider this list of who you are in Christ because he authored and is perfecting your faith.

WHO YOU ARE IN CHRIST

You are his chosen, his precious jewel, his heritage:
Beloved, blameless, and blessed.
You are his possession, his temple, his child,
his masterpiece, and his instrument for noble purposes.

He calls you friend and joint-heir.
He has recruited you as his soldier,
his ambassador, his witness, his co-laborer,
and a minister of his reconciliation.

In Christ, you have been set free from sin,
set free from Satan,

set free from the kingdom of darkness,
and seated in the heavenly places. Amen!

You were purchased by God's Son,
adopted into God's family,
given God's Holy Spirit,
and forgiven of all your trespasses.

By his stripes, you are healed,
by his blood, you are covered,
under his wings, you are sheltered,
in his palm, your name is engraved,
and in his secret place, you are hidden. Selah.

You are a candle in a dark place,
a city set on a hill, and the salt of the earth.

In Christ, you are complete ~ alive ~ a new creation.
Sanctified ~ justified ~ qualified
And one day glorified — Hallelujah!

Delivered ~ included ~ completed ~ protected.
Redeemed and strengthened.
A victor, an overcomer, and MORE. I repeat.
MORE. MORE than a conqueror. *

When you consider that list, you realize there is no universe in which you could possibly be responsible for any of that.

Jesus is the author of your faith. He drew you in. And he didn't draw you to himself only to change his mind and leave you to your own devices.

No, he is the author of your faith and the perfecter of it as well.

For a free color printable of this list, go to RevivalPray.com/free

> FIX YOUR EYES ON JESUS AS:
> PERFECTER OF YOUR FAITH

In all things he is perfecting you, including your difficulties and struggles; your failed plans; your loneliness, frustration, fear, and anxiety. He is working those out and using it all to move you closer to his image.

But there's a problem. You and I are wired to TCB (take care of business) ourselves. You see — although we get the part right about looking to Christ in faith to be saved — somewhere along the way we get it wrong and look to ourselves to persevere and endure.

But the Gospel is not just for salvation; it's for daily sanctification.

In essence — through the Hebrews writer — God says: "Don't fix your eyes on what you can or cannot do. Fix your eyes on what I've already done and am doing in you through the sacrifice of my one and only Son."

So release whatever you've been clinging to for your hope. Give God — the master builder — room to work and raise a framework in your mind and in your heart. Center your thoughts and your hope on his one and only Son: the author and perfecter of your faith.

But wait there's more!

Fixing your eyes on Jesus is not limited to meditating on the work he has done in your life or the change he is perfecting in your life. It extends to the home he is preparing for your soul when all breath leaves your life.

RECENTER YOUR HOPE ON HEAVEN

This hope is not just for one day or some day, it is for **TODAY**.

There's a challenge to overcome here, however. Just like we are so often tempted to leave the Gospel in our past, we relegate the hope of heaven to our **future**.

But the New Testament writers talked often about how an awareness and anticipation of Jesus' return is the key to walking in faith **NOW**. Within the 260 New Testament chapters, the second coming is alluded to more than 300 times. [1]

Jesus himself spoke often of heaven and some of his most powerful parables about heaven were delivered in the week leading up to his death.

John recorded Jesus' words in the upper room the night before his crucifixion. The world of Jesus' disciples was about to disintegrate. Nothing was going to be the same after that night. They were going to lose their bearings and feel like all hope was lost.

Jesus could have said anything to prepare those men for what lay ahead. But consider the words he chose to sustain their hope through the darkest night of their lives to that point.

> *"Do not let your heart be troubled;*
> *believe in God, believe also in Me.*
> *In My Father's house are many dwelling places;*
> *if it were not so, I would have told you;*
> *for I go to prepare a place for you.*
> *If I go and prepare a place for you,*
> *I will come again and receive you to Myself,*
> *that where I am, there you may be also."*
> (John 14:1-3)

The same encouragement is for you. The awareness that this world is not your home and the anticipation of the home in Jesus' presence — if you've responded to him as Savior — are the bookends that help you survive and thrive in the short time he's given you in THIS world.

Centering your hope (or rather recentering it if it has become skewed) and constructing the framework — from which you will view your ups and your downs;

your successes and your failures; your excitement and your fear — builds on this:

- Fix your eyes on Jesus.
- Meditate on how he saved you.
- Submit to the perfection he's working in you.
- View it all through the lens of how he will one day return for you.

Because this world is not your home.
And Jesus IS coming back to take you to the one that is.

———

...

"The power of the Cross is not found in what we do, but in what has been done for us."
— Suzy Eller [2]

...

"Get over yourself! Celebrate Jesus! Don't celebrate you, and don't loathe you. Just focus on Jesus."
—Matt Chandler [3]

...

———

NOTES

1. Henry Thiessen, *Lectures in Systematic Theology* (Grand Rapids, Michigan: Eerdmans, 1989: Originally published 1949), 341.

2. Suzanne Eller, *The Mended Heart* (Grand Rapids, Michigan: Revell, 2014) 148.

3. Matt Chandler, *Living to God* (Flower Mound, Texas: Village Church, 2012) [Sermon transcript here: http://www.tvcresources.net/resource-library/sermons/living-to-god].

THREE
HOPE-FILLED
PRAYER PROMPTS

The word *hope* has been diluted in our English language. We say, "*I hope it doesn't rain*," or "*I hope she's ok*."

But the HOPE we are talking about here is far different. It's the BLESSED HOPE (Titus 2:13) and it's a sure thing. In response to all we've considered, here are three prompts to help direct your thoughts on this blessed hope.

For the first two prompts, we'll use the list from the previous chapter: *Who you are in Christ*. It is reprinted at the end in a format you can use to make notes and record progress through prayer. (Notice some of the similar descriptions have been combined.)

1. THANK JESUS FOR AUTHORING YOUR FAITH.

Pray through the list, thanking Jesus for these precious promises.

Concentrate on the descriptions you are seeing fulfilled already.

Don't fix your eyes on what you can or cannot do. Fix your eyes on what Jesus has already done and is doing in you through his sacrifice.

Save anything on the list that you are struggling with for the next prompt.

2. THANK JESUS FOR PERFECTING YOUR FAITH.

Here we lay before the Lord any descriptions on the list or other "works in progress" you've identified. But instead of focusing on what is lacking, turn the prayer into a praise of provision, believing God is already at work in that area.

Thank him for using your struggles and working those out to move you closer to his image.

End by praying this Scripture back and claiming the promise:

"Being confident of this,
that he who began a good work in you
will carry it on to completion until the day of Christ Jesus."
(Phil. 1:6)

---

3. MEDITATE ON THE HOPE OF HEAVEN.

This world is not your home. Jesus is coming back.

And because we know the destination (or rather, the destiny), we can endure — and even thrive — along the journey.

A friend shared an eye-opening moment with me recently, *"I realized that my 'eternal life' began the day I put my trust in Christ, so I don't have to wait for heaven to have eternal life – it already started!"*

I love that perspective! And perspective can change everything!

As you pray this prompt, return to the words Jesus spoke to his disciples in John 14, and read them as if he were speaking them to you.

Next, contemplate this truth from Rev. 21:4-7:

"He will wipe away every tear from their eyes,
and death shall be no more,
neither shall there be mourning,
nor crying, nor pain anymore,
for the former things have passed away.

And he who was seated on the throne said,
"Behold, I am making all things new."

Also he said,
"Write this down, for these words are trustworthy and true."

And he said to me,
"It is done! I am the Alpha and the Omega,
the beginning and the end.
To the thirsty I will give
from the spring of the water of life
without payment."

Prayer List: Who You Are in Christ

How to use this list:

- Column 1: contains the identifier or promise recorded in Scripture.
- Column 2: place a check if you fully embrace this description and/or promise. Leave it blank if it's still something God is perfecting in you.
- Column 3: record your prayer for God's perfecting work or the progress you've seen as you've prayed for him to bring you to fulfillment regarding the promises not checked off in column 2.

* For a free color printable of this list (suitable for posting) or a copy of the list as formatted for prayer, go to RevivalPray.com/free

IDENTIFIER OR PROMISE FROM SCRIPTURE	✓	PRAYER OR PROGRESS
Beloved and blessed Included and completed		
His chosen and heritage A precious jewel		
Blameless and forgiven Covered by his blood		
His possession; your name is engraved in his palm		
His masterpiece and instrument for noble purposes		
His friend		
His child; joint-heir with Christ Adopted into his family		
Soldier Ambassador		
Minister of his reconciliation His witness		
Qualifed		
Set free from sin; sanctifed and justifed; a new creation		
Set free from Satan and the kingdom of darkness; Delivered		
His temple Given the Holy Spirit		
Healed by his stripes Redeemed and strengthened		
Sheltered under his wings Protected and hidden		
A city set on a hill; a candle Salt of the earth		
Victor and overcomer MORE than a conqueror		

STEP 5: SHORING UP THE STRUCTURE

...

"Thanksgiving is worry's kryptonite."
— Matt Chandler

REINFORCE WITH PRAISE

In the Battle | Through the Valley

During my time living on the Texas Gulf Coast, I learned about building codes designed to ensure that homes withstand hurricane force winds. One of those is hurricane ties — steel straps that reinforce the framing. Engineers know that in the middle of a major storm, structures need extra strength.

The fact that you've built on a stable site — grounded on a solid foundation with a secure framework — means you have a solid structure. However, as you are likely aware, the storms will come. The winds will blow.

There will be times when you need the added strength of praise.

Praise is both a weapon and a refuge.
Scripture records that praise establishes a stronghold against the enemy and silences the foe and avenger. (Ps. 8) It also strengthens your ability to endure and calls upon the God who is worthy of your trust as you go through the valley. (Ps. 18)

In this chapter, we'll look at an instance in Scripture where praise went before God's people in the battle. I'll tell you a personal story of my own experience with the restoring power of praise. We'll end this step by recounting Scriptures that lead you to praise and pray back God's inspired Word over your own struggles and successes.

—————

PRAISE HIM IN THE BATTLE

—————

Consider the story in 2 Chronicles 20 where God's people in Judah were outnumbered. In fact, the war report to King Jehoshaphat detailed, "A great multitude is coming against you from beyond the sea."

The king gathered the people to fast and pray.
After proclaiming God's sovereignty, the king ended with a heart-wrenching cry of dependence:

> *"For we are powerless*
> *against this great horde*
> *that is coming against us.*
> *We do not know what to do,*
> *but our eyes are on you."*
> (2 Chron. 20:12)

God heard that prayer and He answered through a servant:

> *"Do not fear or be dismayed ...*
> *for the battle is not yours but God's."*
> (v 15)

God then told the people to go down against the overwhelming, outnumbering enemy and not hide inside their gates. While the people stood in the wilderness, waiting for the enemy to appear, the king reminded them:

"Put your trust in the Lord your God
and you will be established."
(v 20)

The very next verses tell of people praising God, and some even going before the army singing:

"Give thanks to the Lord,
for His lovingkindness is everlasting."
(v 21)

and then...

"When they began singing and praising,
the Lord set ambushes against (those)
who had come against Judah."
(v 22)

Now, there are many songs of praise proclaiming God's deliverance in the Bible, but this one is different. Here, he delivered them AFTER they began praising him.

This is trust personified — or rather — songified.

Established trust looks like worship and thanksgiving — even before anything you can see changes.

That's reason enough to go find your voice if you've lost it and turn up worship music in the background.

PRAISE HIM THROUGH THE VALLEY

Years ago, I entered a totally unexpected valley; it caught me off guard in every way imaginable.

Initially, I handled it with staunch resolve and faith. But as the issues dragged on and the complications mounted, I became weary and lost my way. I took my eyes off the Savior and only saw the storm. And I lost my "voice" (my ability to write, speak, teach, or encourage others).

When God began to get my attention, he did so by calling me to praise him in the middle of the storm. These are the words I wrote as he began to break through the darkness in my heart:

> "God is writing a new song on my heart – a broken hallelujah of sorts.
> And with that, he is reminding me that when he gives a song, my only response can be to sing.

And so I will sing of the God who doesn't require I hide my crazy from him.
Of the One who is working all things for my good and his glory, even when he seems silent and things seem to be falling apart.

I will sing of my brokenness so that others might hear of the only One who can break through the darkness, mend a heart, and restore a song."

The first part of my voice he rescued was the part I used to praise him. The praise returned my eyes to the Savior and slowly my voice returned fully.

I learned some of the deepest worship occurs in the middle of the broken hallelujah chorus.

Through letting go, I discovered more about the new thing he was doing in my life. He did turn that broken hallelujah into a song others recognized and gave me a place in his plan I could never have dreamed possible. And now I write so others might hear and recognize the song. I could not speak words of comfort had I not first been comforted.

"... the God of all comfort,
who comforts us in all our affliction,

so that we may be able to comfort
those who are in any affliction,
with the comfort with which we ourselves
are comforted by God."
(2 Cor. 1:3-4)

What about you? If you are reading this chapter during a valley experience, I imagine you can relate to this story more than you would like to admit. Maybe you need to start with a broken hallelujah. Maybe you can't launch into a full chorus yet, but can you just trust him to give you one note at a time?

———

...

"When you enter his presence with praise, he enters your circumstances with power."
— Unknown

...

"If we want to experience a closer walk with him, we need only to praise him. His presence will overwhelm us when we choose to get off the normal path and notice the blessings he sends our way each day."
— Lysa Terkeurst [1]

...

NOTES

1. Lysa TerKeurst, *What Happens When Women Walk in Faith* (Eugene, Oregon: Harvest House Publishers, 2005).

FINDING YOUR VOICE BEFORE GOD

~~~

Matt Redman was interviewed about his song, "Blessed Be Your Name," written in the weeks following 9/11:

"It's really a song born out of the whole of life — a realization that we will all face seasons of pain or unease. And in these seasons, we will need to find our voice before God." [1]

Regardless of the season you're in, you must protect your voice before God. Praise is a powerful sustainer, weapon, and joy-builder. It renews your spirit and strengthens your resolve.

PRAISE GOD FOR ALL WE'VE COVERED SO FAR

1-I praise you for your forgiveness and restoration, and your strength working in me that I may forgive others.

2-I praise you for this holy discontent with the status quo in my life.

3-I praise you for your presence and the peace that follows that truth.

4-I praise you for your sovereignty over all creation, your power, and your might; nothing is too hard for you. You are never undone and never outnumbered.

5-I praise you for your work as author and perfecter of my faith, and for this calling to prayer before your throne.

6-I praise you for the hope of heaven and your promise of an eternity spent praising you.

7-I praise you for you are worthy to be praised. Thank you for the gift of worship.

8-I praise you for the joy of my salvation and how you have returned my focus and renewed my thoughts toward you.

9-I praise you ...

♦ **BONUS:** ♦

I created a playlist of praise songs for my ministry site "6 Cries of the Heart." You'll find those and more curated Scripture at 6cries.com.

RETURN GOD'S INSPIRED WORDS AS PRAISE BACK TO HIM

"O Lord, our Lord,
how majestic is your name in all the earth!
You have set your glory above the heavens.

Out of the mouth of babies and infants,
you have established strength
because of your foes,
to still the enemy and the avenger.
When I look at your heavens,
the work of your fingers,
the moon and the stars,
which you have set in place,
what is man that you are mindful of him,
and the son of man that you care for him?"
(Ps. 8:1-4)

"Blessed be the God and Father of our Lord Jesus Christ!
According to his great mercy,
he has caused us to be born again to a living hope through
the resurrection of Jesus Christ from the dead,
to an inheritance that is imperishable, undefiled, and
unfading, kept in heaven for you,
who by God's power are being guarded through faith for a
salvation ready to be revealed in the last time."
(1 Pet. 1:3-5)

"I love you, O Lord, my strength.
The Lord is my rock and my fortress and my deliverer,

108

my God, my rock, in whom I take refuge,
my shield, and the horn of my salvation, my stronghold.
I call upon the Lord, who is worthy to be praised,
and I am saved from my enemies."
(Ps. 18:1-3)

"Now to him who is able to keep you from stumbling
and to present you blameless before the presence of his glory
with great joy,
to the only God, our Savior,
through Jesus Christ our Lord,
be glory, majesty, dominion, and authority,
before all time and now and forever. Amen."
(Jude 1:24-25)

"From the rising of the sun to its setting,
the name of the Lord is to be praised!
The Lord is high above all nations,
and his glory above the heavens!
Who is like the Lord our God,
who is seated on high,
who looks far down
on the heavens and the earth?"
(Ps. 113:3-6)

"'Worthy is the Lamb who was slain,
to receive power and wealth
and wisdom and might
and honor and glory and blessing!'"
And I heard every creature in heaven and on earth
and under the earth and in the sea,
and all that is in them, saying,
"'To him who sits on the throne
and to the Lamb
be blessing and honor and glory
and might forever and ever!'"
(Rev. 5:12-13)

NOTES

prayers

NOTES

1. http://brianmbailey.blogspot.com/2009/03/story-behind-blessed-be-your-name.html

STEP 6:
STANDING ON
THE WALL

...

"... and having done all, to stand firm."
Eph. 6:13b

RESOLVE TO SHINE

---~~~---

How to Live Undaunted

Here at the end of this rebuilding journey, you have a wall to stand on.

With a repentant heart, a steady perspective, a stable foundation, a hope fixed on Jesus and the promise of heaven, and armed with the power of praise, you have rebuilt. Your mind is renewed. You have reclaimed ground the enemy had taken. There's one last thing you need to know:

You don't experience revival just for yourself. You're called to inspire and prompt others. **Shine, stand, and withstand.**

Perhaps this is the moment for which YOU were made. There's a dark world out there, but light shines brightest against the darkness. And when light shines, others SEE.

Jesus called believers light. He said they are a city on a hill (Matt. 5:14-16). God has placed his all-powerful light within the lives of his people. Until Jesus returns to take you home, you are a light-bearer for such a time as this.

The enemy would have you believe your tiny little candle can't hold a candle to the heavy sulphur-laden blackness that is wrapping its tentacles around the world. **But that's a lie.**

The truth is this:
As a believer, your light comes from THE Light and greater is HE that is in you than he that is in the world. (1 Jn 4:4)

Think about how the beginning began (Gen. 1).
Darkness was over the earth.
Until.

Until God spoke.

And once he spoke, there was light.

And it was GOOD.

And God separated the light from the darkness.

The one who lights your heart is the one who brought light from absolute darkness.

He CREATED light.

There is no darkness HIS light cannot drive out.

Paul calls out the deceiver, saying he has:

> *"blinded the minds of the unbelievers,*
> *to keep them from seeing*
> *the light of the gospel of the glory of Christ."*
> (2 Cor. 4:4)

There's a world full of blind unbelievers out there who need your little light to shine. They need you to look different and react differently and cause them to ask "Why?"

But equally so, there's a battalion of weary warriors who believe but are battling discouragement. They sit on the sidelines with only a flicker, hoping someone will fan the flame so their cold hearts will beat with warm passion again.

I challenge you to resolve to be the light on a stand, not the one under a bushel.

With that in mind, here is one last story of encouragement from the life of Daniel.

HOW TO SHINE AND STAND AND LIVE UNDAUNTED

The story of Daniel in the lions' den is taught as one of the greatest single acts of courage found in the Old Testament.

However, think about this: aside from when Daniel explains to the king why he survived, there isn't a single verse describing his experience in the den.

Daniel is the author of this account, and under the Spirit's inspiration, he chose to include this incident as simply a **footnote** at the end of his life, **void** of details. The emphasis is on his convictions prior to the den and the resulting glory given to God by the king when it was over.

How Daniel lived his life that got him thrown in the den is the real story here. From **beginning** to **end**, he lived undaunted.

He both survived and thrived in the middle of a pagan culture holding to his commitment, grounded in confidence, and compelled by conviction.

1-UNDAUNTED COMMITMENT

From the beginning of chapter one, you see Daniel resolving to solely honor the only sovereign worthy of his worship.

Ripped from his home and taken into Babylonian captivity as a young teen, he was placed in the king's court to be groomed for the king's service. He was served food sacrificed to idols, and eating that food would have been synonymous with honoring the false gods.

Daniel and three of his friends refused to participate and it all worked out (1:9).

As a teen, Daniel *"purposed in his heart"* to refuse defiling himself with the king's food. (1:8)

As an old man, Daniel *"continued ... praying before his God"* after the king signed the law forbidding it. (6:10)

His decision to continue to pray in his EIGHTIES, despite the king's edict, was propelled by the same conviction that caused him to refuse the idol's food as a TEEN. He was committed to honoring God above all else.

Daniel knew it was God who granted favor and God who would sustain him if favor was rescinded.

2-UNDAUNTED CONFIDENCE

This commitment produced a confidence that held fast despite captivity.

Caught in the backwash of God's judgment on his people and living in a hostile nation, Daniel and his friends could have chosen to place their confidence in the new government. They could easily have reasoned:

"When in Babylon, why not do as the Babylonians?"
"God doesn't need us to defend him, and we have

to fend for ourselves."

"We must do whatever preserves what little freedom we have left."

Other Jewish captives compromised (1:13) but not Daniel and his three friends. As young teens, they were powerless, and yet still unafraid of the powerful.

Because their confidence was grounded in God's sovereignty, they did not order their actions in order to gain favor. They didn't compromise their beliefs just to please a politician.

They experienced true freedom of religion because their worship was not beholden to a government's decrees. And when Daniel's three friends stood for God, declaring they wouldn't bow — regardless — they testified with their very lives and God got the glory. (3:28)

Undaunted confidence sounded like this: "But. If. Not." (3:18)

3-UNDAUNTED CONVICTIONS

As Daniel recorded the events of his life, he appeared to be weaving an underlying message that in essence said, "To understand what I **did**, understand what I **knew**."

The second sentence he penned about captivity declared it was the Lord who allowed it to happen, indicating Daniel knew God was in control of who was in control.

Early on, he interpreted King Nebuchadnezzar's statue vs. rock dream. The underlying message was this: **rock wins.**(2:44)

Later, when Nebuchadnezzar's successor Belshazzar offered Daniel the third highest position in the kingdom, Daniel responded, *"Keep your gifts ..."* (5:17)

And at the time Daniel stood up to the king's edict (refusing to refuse to pray), King Darius was planning to promote Daniel over his entire kingdom (6:3). This didn't factor in for a second in his decision. His place in the **empire** never trumped his place in the **kingdom**.

He was convinced beyond a doubt that God was sovereign over all. This conviction compelled him to both take a **STAND** and continue to **KNEEL**. He was never beholden to earthly power and did not fear losing it.

So long before the stone was ever rolled over the den, Daniel's convictions were sealed in the **ROCK**.

4-UNDAUNTED COURAGE

We all read the end of Daniel 6 with a little yearning. The hero held to his faith and God held the hero. The story was passed down through the ages and held up as an example of undaunted courage.

Now, we don't wish for the near-death experience, but we do want to do something worth experiencing with our lives. We want to see God come through with a display of power and we want to display courage worthy of a story.

But Daniel's real story is the courage lived out in his commitment, confidence, and convictions.

His DAILY prayers.
His DAILY work.
His DAILY choices.

His life was so consistent with his beliefs that those who sought to destroy him could find nothing to target but his faith. So it must be with us, friend. You and I don't have to "dare to be a Daniel."

> We dare to live the ordinary, mundane, daily life of integrity.
> We dare to start over today when we failed yesterday.
> We dare to hold fast to hope when all around seems hopeless.

Undaunted courage is rarely seen and observed by others.

> It's the recurring commitment to honor God *no matter what.*
> It's the routine choice to believe he's there, even when you can't see him working.
> It's the daily decision to line up your actions with your convictions and fall again to your knees when it still feels like your prayers are hitting the ceiling.

*Courage begins with "purposing in your heart,"
long before you encounter a den of lions.*

...

"God is the God of "right now." He doesn't want you sitting around regretting yesterday. Nor does He want you wringing your hands and worrying about the future. He wants you focusing on what He is saying to you and putting in front of you ... right now."
— Priscilla Shirer [1]

...

"Courage is contagious. When a brave man takes a stand, the spines of others are often stiffened."
—Billy Graham [2]

...

NOTES

1. Priscilla Shirer, *Discerning the Voice of God* (Chicago, Illinois: Moody Publishers, 2007).

2. http://www.crosswalk.com/faith/spiritual-life/inspiring-quotes/40-courageous-quotes-from-billy-graham.html

THREE PRAYERS TO SHINE AND STAND

‒‒‒‒‒〜〜‒‒‒‒

From my experience, I know anyone resolving to make a change or make a difference will come up against an enemy hell-bent on stopping such forward progress. We began this journey talking about how the word revival likely makes our enemy shudder. As you close out these steps, it's vital that you hear this warning: he won't let you take your light into the night without a fight.

But friend, our God is GREATER. And he is the one who can add fuel to the fire he's ignited in you and shore you up to stand. Don't close this book without praying these three prayers back to the one who led you here to begin with.

I. ASK GOD TO SHOW YOU HOW AND WHERE TO SHINE.

"For God, who said,
"Light shall shine out of darkness,"
is the One who has shone in our hearts
to give the Light of the knowledge
of the glory of God in the face of Christ.
But we have this treasure in earthen vessels,
so that the surpassing greatness of the power
will be of God and not from ourselves."
(2 Cor. 4:6-7)

"You are the light of the world.
A city set on a hill cannot be hidden.
Nor do people light a lamp and put it under a basket,
but on a stand,
and it gives light to all in the house.

In the same way, let your light shine before others,
so that they may see your good works
and give glory to your Father who is in heaven."
(Matt. 5:14-16)

> ## 2. ASK GOD TO EMBOLDEN YOUR COURAGE TO STAND ON YOUR KNEES.

When I taught children the Ephesians armor of God through the decades, we worked through six pieces listed in Scripture: belt of truth, breastplate of righteousness, peace shoes, shield of faith, salvation helmet, and Sword of the Spirit. It hasn't been until recently that I realized we were always missing a seventh (and critical) piece of the puzzle, er armor: prayer.

Notice how many times both prayer (also known as petition) and the call to stand / be strong are included in this short passage. As you read and observe, ask God to send this truth from his Word straight to the center of your mind, your heart, and your soul.

"Finally, be __strong__ in the Lord
and in the __strength__ of His might.
Put on the full armor of God,

129

*so that you will be able to **<u>stand firm</u>***
against the schemes of the devil.

...

Therefore, take up the full armor of God,
so that you will be able to resist in the evil day,
*and having done everything, to **<u>stand firm</u>**.*

***<u>Stand firm</u>** therefore,*
having girded your loins with truth,

...

*With all **<u>prayer</u>** and **<u>petition</u>***
***<u>pray</u>** at all times in the Spirit,*
and with this in view,
be on the alert with all perseverance
*and **<u>petition</u>** for all the saints,*
*and **<u>pray</u>** on my behalf ..."*
(Eph. 6:10-11;13-14;18-19a)

3. ASK GOD TO STRENGTHEN YOUR RESOLVE TO WITHSTAND

Just like the story of Daniel, ask God for the courage to purpose in your heart day by day. Ask him to fill in your gaps and point you to the truth you'll need to sustain you if — or rather when — you land in the lions' den.

And remember:

Courage doesn't always sound like a roar. Sometimes it sounds like a quiet voice at the end of the day saying, "I will try again tomorrow."

"And let steadfastness have its full effect,
that you may be perfect and complete,
lacking in nothing.

...

Blessed is the man
who remains steadfast under trial,
for when he has stood the test
he will receive the crown of life,
which God has promised
to those who love him."

(James 1:4,12)

Revival

NOTES

THOUGHTS

prayers

FINAL THOUGHTS

I don't know what revival will look like in your life. It's different for all of us.

It may be the strength to withstand where you are.
It may be an overwhelming sense of God's calling for your next step.
It may be a subtle whisper that envelopes you with peace.
It may be an overflowing heart that cannot stop praising his precious name in the middle of your storm.

Whatever it is, it will continue to grow and morph as you continually submit in prayer grounded on God's Word.

This is not over; it has only just begun.

Revive us, Oh Lord!

A FINAL PRAYER

———————

Dear Jesus,

Take my light.
It is yours. It came from you.

Wherever my feet go, my words land, or my keyboard sends, use me to dispel darkness today.

Help me to shine for you so others may see YOUR LIGHT and have the eyes of their heart enlightened and filled with HOPE.

Show me how to point others toward the TRUTH.

Open my own eyes to see the ETERNAL and give me strength to stand against the unseen who would seek to blow out my little light.

Hallelujah, Maranatha, and Amen!

...

———————

Quotes on Dividers not included in chapter end notes:

Introduction: [1]
Step 1 [2]
Step 2 [3]
Step 3 [4]
Step 5 [5]

NOTES

1. Marks of Revival, Revival Commentary, v. 1, n. 1. accessed here on June 4, 2017: http://www.evanwiggs.com/revival/manifest/ marks.html

2. Charles H. Spurgeon, *The Complete Works of C.H. Spurgeon* (United States: Delmarva Publications, 2013), sermon 329.

3. Carey Nieuwhof, "5 Predictions about the U.S. Presidential Election." Blog at *careynieuwhof.com*. Oct. 24, 2016. Accessed June 4, 2017. https://careynieuwhof.com/5-predictions-about-the-us-presidential-election/

4. Dr. J. Vernon McGee, *Ephesians* (Thomas Nelson, 1995).

5. Matt Chandler, *To Live is Christ* (Colorado Spring, CO: David C Cook, 2013), 176.

ABOUT THE AUTHOR

CHRISTI GEE

Making Life and Words Count

...

Christi Gee is a listener, speaker, writer, and forever student of God's Word.

She began teaching the Bible while she was still a teen. Through the decades, she led children's ministries and wrote church and Christian school curriculum on subjects such as worldview, apologetics, and chronological scope and sequences.

While still working as a marketing director at Liberty University, she began blogging and now reaches thousands each week through her work at ChristiGee.com.

Through the years, her professional career in marketing and her volunteer activities in ministry always took a back seat to her highest calling: raising her three children.

Now that they are launched and the nest is empty, she has begun branching out, opening doors to find the next thing. Releasing her first book is her own first step into this new chapter of life.

Although Texans for over four decades, she and her husband, Eddie, now live on the East Coast.

Find out more about her speaking or marketing consulting services here: christigee.com/work-with-me/

Connect with her in these places:

Facebook: @ChristiGeeDotCom
Instagram: @ChristiLGee
Twitter: @ChristiLGee

#RevivalPrayBook

How you can
help

I don't take it lightly that in a busy world, you chose to welcome in these whispers.

Since this book is self-published, reviews matter even more than normal. They are the MAIN avenue for catching others' attention.

Even if you didn't buy the book on Amazon, you can still leave a review on the book's sales page.

We also need to build up reviews on Goodreads.com

Thank you in advance for taking the time to help send this message forward!

REVIVALPRAY.COM

FOR DISCOUNTED BULK ORDERS OR TO CONTACT CHRISTI ABOUT HOSTING A RETREAT CENTERED ON THIS TOPIC, GO TO: REVIVALPRAY.COM

The bonus downloads, including the Workbook & Prayer Journal are available at RevivalPray.com/free.

Made in the USA
Middletown, DE
30 April 2018